# EARTH SCIENCE LIBRARY
# DESERTS
## MARTYN BRAMWELL

Franklin Watts

London · New York · Toronto · Sydney

© 1987 Franklin Watts

First published in Great Britain by
Franklin Watts
12a Golden Square
London W1

First published in the USA by
Franklin Watts Inc.
387 Park Avenue South
New York, N.Y. 10016

First published in Australia by
Franklin Watts Australia
14 Mars Road
Lane Cove
NSW 2066

UK ISBN: 0 86313 525 0
US ISBN: 0-531-10355-2
Library of Congress Catalog Card
No: 86-51409

Printed in Belgium

Designed by Ben White

Picture research by Mick
Alexander

Illustrations:
Chris Forsey
Tim Hayward

Photographs:
Ardea 7*r*, 22*r*, 23*l*, 28*l*
Bruce Coleman 10, 14*l*, 16*r*, 17*l*,
 21
Robert Harding 1, 11, 13*b*, 15*r*, 25,
 26*r*
Eric & David Hosking 19*t*
Frank Lane 7*l*, 13*t*, 15*l*, 16*l*, 17*r*,
 20, 29*l*
Seaphot 5, 9, 28*r*, 29*r*
ZEFA *back cover*, 4, 8, 12, 14*r*,
 19*b*, 22*l*, 23*r*, 24, 26*l*, 27

# EARTH SCIENCE LIBRARY
# DESERTS

## Contents

# The arid lands

To many people, the word **desert** conjours up a picture of rolling sand dunes, a blazing yellow Sun, camel trains and palm-fringed **oases**. And there is nothing wrong with that picture – except that it is only one small part of the story.

Sand deserts form only a small proportion of the world's **arid** (dry) lands. Many deserts are vast expanses of flat stony ground, covered with coarse **scrub** vegetation. Others are mountainous regions of shattered rock, with barely a leaf or twig to be seen. Each type is formed by a particular combination of temperature, rainfall, wind and geology. There are hot deserts and cold deserts; deserts where rain has never been seen and deserts with up to 30 cm (12 in) of rain a year. The arid lands are surprisingly varied. They are home to millions of people, more than 5,000 kinds of animal, and an enormous number of specialized plants.

△ The "sand seas" and oases of the Sahara in Tunisia are typical of the kind of desert made familiar in countless films and adventure stories.

▷ Nearly a quarter of the Earth's surface receives less than 50 cm (20 in) of rain a year and is classified as arid. But half of this (an area the size of Africa) is desert, with less than 25 cm (10 in) of rain a year.

1  American Desert
2  Atacama Desert
3  Patagonian Desert
4  Sahara Desert
5  Arabian Desert
6  Turkestan Desert
7  Iran/Afghanistan Desert
8  Gobi Desert
9  Namib Desert
10  Kalahari Desert
11  Australian Desert

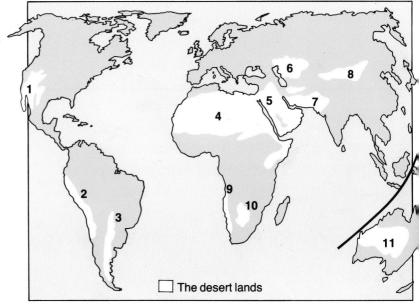

The desert lands

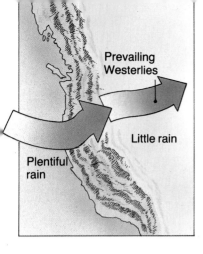

Prevailing Westerlies

Little rain

Plentiful rain

△ The **Westerly** winds that carry moisture into the west side of North America lose most of their moisture over the Rockies. Little rain reaches the desert areas or the dry grasslands that lie farther to the north.

▽ As moist air rises, it cools down and can no longer hold as much water. The upwind side of a mountain therefore receives plenty of rain, while the downwind side (the **rain shadow**) stays dry.

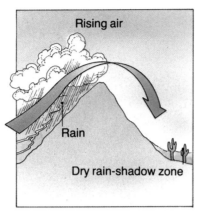

Rising air

Rain

Dry rain-shadow zone

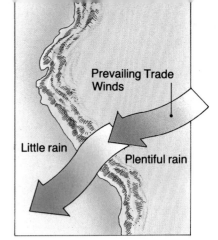

Prevailing Trade Winds

Little rain

Plentiful rain

△ The **Trade Winds** that carry moisture into South America from the Atlantic lose their moisture over the Amazon rainforest and the eastern slopes of the Andes range. The narrow coastal region is a cold dry desert.

One of the most difficult things to imagine is the sheer size of the desert lands. The Sahara alone covers more than 9 million square km (3½ million square miles), which makes it more than 16 times the size of France – Europe's largest country.

Some deserts owe their existence mainly to mountain ranges that lie across the path of the **prevailing winds**. As the air is forced to rise over the mountains, it is cooled, and the moisture it carries falls as rain. By the time the air flows down the other side, it is warm and dry. Far from producing any rain, it even soaks up what little moisture there is in the desert soil.

The great deserts of North Africa, Arabia, Afghanistan and Australia lie near the **tropics**, north and south of the equator. These are zones of high **atmospheric pressure**, where warm dry air sinks towards the Earth's surface. There are few clouds and very little rain. The days are searingly hot, while night temperatures plunge to near zero.

△ Spectacular desert scenery in Monument Valley, Arizona, USA. Castle-like **buttes** and flat-topped **mesas** are the remnants of an ancient landscape, worn away by the wind and by violent desert storms.

5

# Shifting sands

As strong winds blow across the surface of a desert, fine dust is picked up and carried high into the air. It may be swept along for hundreds of kilometres before being dropped. In ages past, thick layers of this material – called **loess** – have built up in some parts of the world. The fertile plains of northern China, for example, consist of loess carried there from the Gobi Desert.

Coarser, heavier, sand grains are swept along closer to the ground. They soon become rounded and highly polished. As they blow along, they form sand dunes of various shapes and sizes. The grains are swept up the windward, or upwind, side of the dune and tumble down the lee side, where the wind slackens and swirls into an eddy.

▽ There are four main types of sand dune:
1 Transverse dunes
2 Barchans
3 Seif dunes
4 Star dunes
There are also several other types, such as whaleback dunes. These are long, flat-topped ridges up to 160 km (100 miles) long, 5 km (3 miles) wide and 45 m (150 ft) high. They are similar to seif dunes, but are smooth and rounded, without any steep slip-faces.

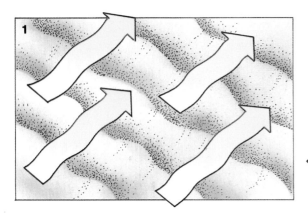

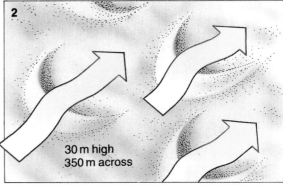

30 m high
350 m across

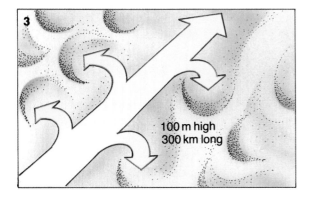

100 m high
300 km long

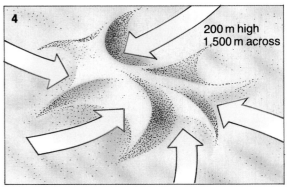

200 m high
1,500 m across

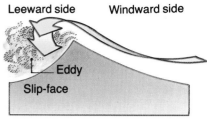

Leeward side     Windward side

Eddy

Slip-face

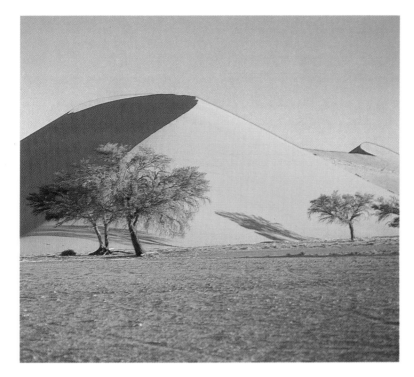

◁This huge sand dune, photographed in the Namib Desert of southwest Africa, is moving from right to left as we look at it. Note the steep, slightly hollowed-out shape of the slip-face, partly hidden by shadows.

As more and more sand is moved from the gently sloping windward side to the steeper leeward side, the whole dune moves slowly forward in the direction of the wind. In some desert regions, whole oases, and even small towns, have been engulfed by moving sand dunes.

The shape and size of the dunes depends on the strength of the wind and on how constantly it blows from one direction. Steady, gentle, winds produce *transverse dunes* rather like the ripples on a beach, but bigger. Stronger winds are likely to produce crescent-shaped *barchans*, whose "horns" point downwind. Strong winds from one direction combined with strong cross-winds may produce long *seif dunes*, which may stretch for hundreds of kilometres and reach heights of over 200 m (650 ft). Where wind direction is more variable, the swirling gusts and eddies may build large irregularly shaped *star dunes*.

△Cross-bedded sandstones are the "fossilized" remains of ancient desert sand dunes. The curved lines are old slip-faces, and the bigger divisions mark where sets of dunes have been piled one on top of another by the ever-changing wind.

# Deserts shaped by water

△ Algodones Dunes in southern California – the Sahara of the United States. Even in this blisteringly hot desert there is enough water under the surface to support deep-rooted desert plants. There are even a few **salt lakes**, each surrounded by scores of gullies and **arroyos** – the dry stream beds that fill briefly after desert storms.

▷ When almost horizontal layers of **sedimentary** rocks such as sandstone, limestone and shale are worn away by river erosion in a desert area, the result is a landscape of steps, platforms and deep canyons.

The *cuesta* is a sharp step formed by a band of hard rock. Mesas are flat-topped remnants of earlier levels, now almost worn away. Buttes are smaller remnants, often worn into pinnacles and tower shapes.

The most obvious feature of any desert is its dryness, yet few deserts are completely without rain – and, surprisingly perhaps, it is rain and running water that carve the desert landscape.

The driest place on Earth is in the Atacama Desert, around Calama in Chile. This region is believed to have gone for 400 years with no more than about 1 mm (0.05 in) of rain a year. But in 1972 the region was struck by a violent thunderstorm. Torrential rain poured on to the Sun-baked ground, rushing down the hillsides in muddy torrents. Bridges and roads were swept away, mines were flooded, and the town of Calama was surrounded by flood waters.

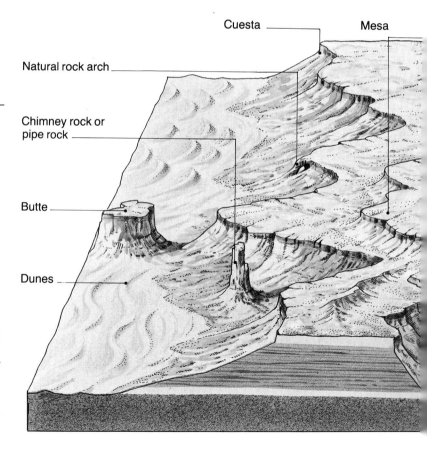

Cuesta · Mesa · Natural rock arch · Chimney rock or pipe rock · Butte · Dunes

Many deserts, by contrast, receive up to 25 cm (10 in) of rain a year. Spread evenly over several months, that amount of water would support grassland, and even some trees. But the clue to the desert landscape is that the rain comes in short, violent downpours. The hard earth cannot soak up the water as it does in gentler climates, so the water rushes over the surface, loaded with sand, stones and even boulders. Deep channels and **gullies** are cut into the landscape, and the sand and stones are swept out on to the lower ground in huge **outwash fans**.

In **temperate** regions, **erosion** – the wearing away of the land – is a slow and continuous process. In deserts it occurs in short sharp bursts, but the effects on the landscape are dramatic.

△ The enormous power of a **flash flood** is clear from this deep canyon in the Negev Desert of Israel.

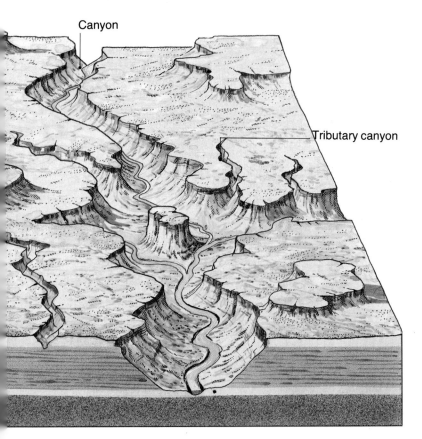

Canyon

Tributary canyon

◁ If a desert area has been raised up by movements of the Earth's **crust**, most of its rivers' cutting power is directed downwards as the rivers try to get back to their old levels. The result is that rivers in such areas cut sheer-sided **gorges**. One of the most famous is the Grand Canyon, a 1,900 m (6,250 ft) gash cut through the sedimentary rocks of the Arizona Desert by the Colorado River.

9

# Rock spires and arches

The main force of desert erosion is the scouring effect of running water laden with sand and stones. But water can erode in other ways too.

Rain falling through the air absorbs carbon dioxide gas, and this makes it slightly acidic. Some minerals will dissolve in water, but they dissolve even more easily in acidic water. One of the most common minerals is calcium carbonate, found in limestone. Over long periods of time, limestone rocks are slowly dissolved and washed away. Some sandstones, too, are affected because in many types the grains of silica sand are cemented together by carbonate minerals. When these are dissolved, the sand grains are loosened and the rock surface becomes soft and crumbly.

Even some of the minerals in **granite** can be dissolved in this way, leaving the rock surface weak and easily worn away by wind and water.

▽ These chimney rocks in Monument Valley, Arizona, are the tattered remnants of buttes. Earlier still, they were part of a flat-topped mesa, like the one in the background. Water erosion has done most of the work, but the sandstone pillars will finally be reduced to dust by the grinding action of sand blown by the wind.

△Window Rock in Arizona is the result of millions of years of erosion by water and wind. Like many such windows and arches, it may have started off as a knob of slightly harder limestone jutting out into the path of a river. At first the river would have run round the obstruction in a loop, but eventually it would have broken through. Since then, rain and wind have put the finishing touches to a natural masterpiece.

◁The bizarre landscape of Bryce Canyon in Utah is the work of rain, snow and wind on thick layers of limestone coloured by manganese and iron minerals. In Paiute Indian legend, the rock pillars are warriors, turned to stone by the Spirits because they fell into dishonourable ways.

11

# Stony deserts

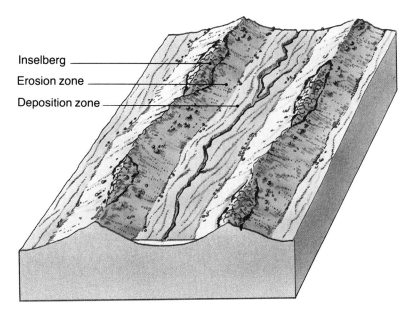

Inselberg
Erosion zone
Deposition zone

◁This illustration shows the main features in a desert landscape carved from hard volcanic rocks or layers of very hard sedimentary rock. The bare rocky summits are being broken up by constant temperature changes and by the action of wind and rain. On the steep slopes below, rock fragments are being carried slowly downhill, and at the bottom lies the zone of **deposition**, where the worn-down fragments come to rest.

Because the air over desert regions is very dry, it is rare for clouds to develop. One important effect of this is that the deserts receive very little rain. The other is that there is an enormous difference between day and night temperatures. By day the air temperature may soar to 50°C (122°F), while bare rock surfaces may reach well over 80°C (176°F). At night, with no cloud cover to trap any of the Earth's stored heat, the temperature will usually fall at least to 20°C (68°F) and may even plunge to near freezing.

The effect of this on the surface rocks is quite literally shattering. Any object will expand – that is, get bigger – when heated and contract again on cooling. But most rocks consist of several different minerals, all of which expand and contract at different rates. The constant heating and cooling, day after day, eventually cracks the mineral crystals and weakens the rock. Wind and rain complete the job of wearing the rock away.

△Typical desert scenery in Jordan. The jagged rocks of an inselberg stand out above a boulder-strewn slope of shattered rock fragments. Note the hardy vegetation that reveals the presence of moisture in the *wadi*.

The kinds of desert scenery produced in areas of volcanic rocks like granite are very different from those produced in areas of flat sedimentary rocks. Instead of horizontal surfaces broken up by steep cliffs and deep gorges, the land is more irregular and hilly. Ridges of hard rock stand out in the landscape, their summits topped by jagged outcrops of rock called **inselbergs**. Below them lie steep slopes of broken rock, slowly being worn down by wind and water. Gradually the fragments slip downhill or are washed down by flash floods, until eventually they come to rest in the hollows between the ridges.

This kind of landscape is common throughout North Africa and the deserts of Arabia, Iran and Afghanistan, and the different types of surface are often known by their North African names. Bare rock ridges and mountains are called *hammadas*, flat lowlands of gravel and stone are *regs*, and sand-dune "seas" are called *ergs*.

△ Rocky semi-desert covered with scattered coarse grass and scrub vegetation is typical of the Great Karroo Desert in South Africa.

▽ Huge daily temperature changes can cause enormous slabs of rock to split away from granite outcrops.

13

# The power of the wind

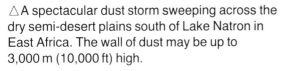
△A spectacular dust storm sweeping across the dry semi-desert plains south of Lake Natron in East Africa. The wall of dust may be up to 3,000 m (10,000 ft) high.

Although water is the main force that creates the mountains, valleys and plains of desert regions, the wind also plays a great part in shaping the landscape. Small-scale features such as sand dunes and the strange-shaped rocks found in many desert areas are often sculpted by the wind.

Sand storms and dust storms are common in all desert regions, and their effects can often be felt hundreds of kilometres away. On numerous occasions pink dust or pink rain has fallen on parts of Italy and France – and even as far north as Britain. The strange colouring is now known to be caused by fine red dust picked up by storms over the Sahara Desert and carried northwards to Europe by high-level winds.

△The traditional clothing of the desert tribes of the Sahara covers the body from head to toe. The loose-fitting garments keep the wearer cool and protected from the blowing sand. As well as being practical, the headdress has become part of the culture and tradition of the Tuareg people. Even their name means people of the veil.

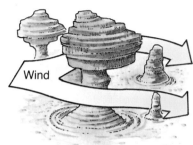

The desert is full of surprising shapes. The white domes of **calcareous** rock (*left*) in the Great Sand Sea of Egypt, and the famous Mushroom Rock in Death Valley, California (*below*) are beautiful examples of wind erosion.

Wind

Fine dust may be carried high into the air, but sand is much heavier and is seldom lifted higher than about 2 m (6 ft) from the ground. Even so, winds that blow for long periods at 60 to 90 km/h (40 to 60 mph) can move enormous amounts of sand from place to place. Large dunes are constantly shaped and reshaped, while other parts of the desert are blown completely clear of sand and left as bare polished rock. Even individual pebbles may be worn into strange, flat-sided shapes by windblown sand. They are called *ventifacts*, and are often sold as tourist souvenirs.

Where large rocks or rock pinnacles stand alone, their bases are often worn away by sand blowing against them. Wooden posts have even less chance. In desert regions, telegraph wires are often brought down when the wooden poles carrying them are "sawn" through about a metre (3 ft) from the ground by the rasping of the sand.

# Plant life of the desert

Deserts are the harshest and most unfriendly of all Earth's **habitats**, yet they are home to a huge variety of plants. Each one has modified, or adapted in some way to cope with the extreme conditions of heat and drought.

The biggest problem of all, of course, is the shortage of water. Nothing can live without it, and so the plants of the desert have developed a number of "survival strategies" to overcome the problem. These strategies fall into two main types. The plants can either avoid the worst periods of drought entirely, or they can fight the desert – using a whole range of adaptations to reach what water there is, store some of it and avoid wasting any of it.

△ Most members of the *Cereus* family are tall cacti with thick fleshy stems, but the night-flowering dwarf type stores its moisture in a specially modified root, rather like a turnip.

△ The *Welwitschia* of the Namib Desert is one of the strangest desert plants. It grows extremely slowly, produces new plants only rarely, and lives to a great age.

◁ The Namib Desert in bloom after rain. Flowering plants are an important source of food for many desert animals.

△ This hedgehog cactus in Arizona is in an ideal position, as dew and rain will collect in the cracks and holes of its rock ledge.

△ A plump organ-pipe cactus in Arizona. Like many cacti, this species has a ribbed and grooved stem that can expand and contract like a concertina. This enables the plant to fill up its tissues with water whenever it rains.

Many flowering plants avoid the worst periods of drought by lying dormant, as seeds, in the dry soil. When the rains come, the seeds germinate at once. Within days the desert bursts into a blaze of colour as the flowers open. Insects arrive as if from nowhere to feed on the flowers, and to **pollinate** them at the same time. After a few short weeks the flowers are gone. New seeds have been scattered on the dry ground, and the desert is bare once more. The flowers have won – by getting their timing just right and by compressing their whole life cycle into a short burst of activity.

The "fighters" use a whole variety of tricks. Long, tough roots probe deep into the ground for water. Specialized stems and roots are used as water-storage containers. Hairy leaves and tough leathery surfaces help to cut down water loss, while an armory of thorns and spikes keeps away all but the most determined plant-eaters.

△ The aloe stores water in its thick fleshy leaves. Water loss by **evaporation** is kept down by the leaves' tough waxy outer skin.

# Animals of the desert

Just as plants have become specially adapted to live in the desert, so too have many animals. Some have special modifications of their bodies, some rely on special kinds of behaviour or lifestyle, some use a combination of both. But whatever method the animal uses, its main aims are to avoid overheating and to **conserve** the precious water in its body.

Drinking water is in very short supply, so the larger animals must stay within reach of water holes or streams. Some of the smaller animals, however, like rats and mice, rarely drink. They get all the water they need from the seeds and shoots they eat. Others, like lizards, snakes, spiders and hedgehogs, are hunters, and they get their water from their insect and animal **prey**. Most of these animals reduce waste by passing only tiny amounts of very concentrated **urine**.

▽ The drawing shows some of the animals of the American Desert (although in real life you would never see so many so close together). While a gopher shelters from the heat, a kangaroo rat has a narrow escape from a rattlesnake that has tracked it by sensing its body heat. The gila monster, a poison-fanged lizard, rests in the shade, but the green collared lizard has just woken up and is warming its body in the Sun. Like all lizards and snakes, it is cold-blooded and must use the Sun's heat to warm itself before it can go about its activities.

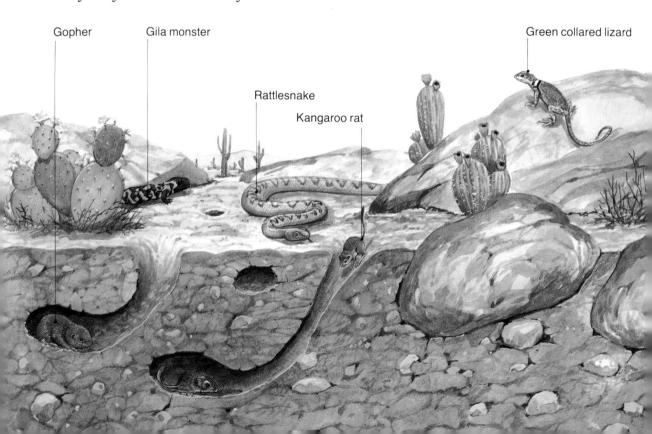

Gopher    Gila monster    Green collared lizard

Rattlesnake

Kangaroo rat

The scorching Sun is an animal's biggest enemy, so many desert dwellers are **nocturnal**, that is, they move about mainly at night. By day they shelter in burrows, in crevices under rocks, or beneath vegetation. Those that do move around by day usually hop, or run on tip-toe, keeping their bodies high off the scorching sand. Even some snakes – the sidewinders – can move along with most of the body clear of the ground.

It is interesting to see how the process of evolution has often produced the same adaptation in animals on different continents. The kangaroo rat of America, jerboa of Asia and gerbil of Africa are almost carbon copies, with long back legs for hopping and long tails for balance. The American kit fox and African fennec fox are another matching pair of desert specialists.

△ The fennec fox's large ears are an adaptation for getting rid of excess body heat.

▽ Camels cannot survive without any water, but they can go for weeks without drinking if they have plenty of green vegetation to feed on.

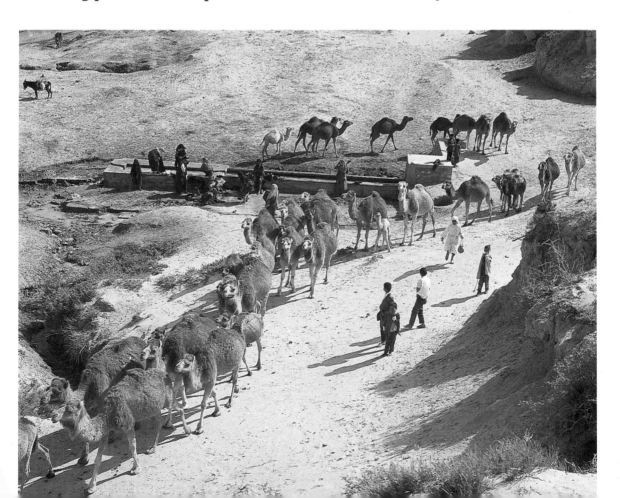

# Versatile desert birds

◁The gila woodpecker is a real specialist. It makes its home in the huge saguaro cacti of Arizona and Mexico. To avoid losing water, the cactus lines the inside of the nest hole with a tough waterproof skin.

△The whippoorwill survives the bitter winter cold of the American Desert by hibernating. The bird goes into a kind of deep sleep. Its body temperature falls from its usual 38°C (100°F) to about 16°C (60°F) and it lives off its reserves of stored body fat.

Birds need far less modification than animals do for life in the desert. Feathers provide their main protection against the fierce heat. They are such efficient insulators that even when the surface of a bird's plumage is almost too hot to touch, the bird's skin can remain at its normal body temperature of about 40°C (104°F). The secret lies in the tiny pockets of air trapped under the plumage. Air is a very poor conductor of heat, so the bird has its own natural, portable, heat shield.

Even so, no animal can risk losing too much moisture by staying out too long in the desert Sun. Most birds feed during the early morning and evening, sheltering in the shade of rocks or vegetation during the hottest part of the day.

Some birds are able to obtain all the water they need from the seeds, berries and insects they eat, but others need to drink regularly. Flight gives them a great advantage over animals, for they can travel long distances in search of water. Some arid-land birds, such as the parakeets of Australia, travel far and wide across the dry plains of the **outback** in huge flocks, following the desert rains.

On the other hand, many desert birds have given up flight in favour of living on the ground. The biggest of all, the ostrich of Africa and the rhea of South America, cannot fly at all, while many others fly only when danger threatens. Many of these birds are plant-eaters but some have become highly specialized, fleet-footed hunters of lizards, snakes and large insects.

△ The American roadrunner is a ground-dwelling hunter that preys on lizards, mice, snakes, small birds and insects. It can sprint at 40 km/h (25 mph), and kills its prey with a single stab of its sharp bill.

◁ At dawn and dusk in the Namib and Kalahari Deserts, Namaqua sandgrouse leave their nests and fly up to 80 km (50 miles) to a water hole. After drinking, the bird soaks its feathers – and uses them like a sponge to carry water back to its thirsty chicks who "nibble" the wet feathers.

21

# Hunters, herdsmen and traders

The human body has no special adaptations for desert life, but people have lived in deserts for thousands of years by adapting their way of life to the harsh conditions there.

Food and water are scarce in the desert, and so many desert people are **nomads** – that is, they do not have a permanent home. Instead, they keep moving, living in one place for a while and then moving on. The simplest lifestyle is that of the hunter-gatherers like the Bushmen of the Kalahari and the Aborigines of Australia. They live on a diet of roots, shoots, berries and insects, gathered from the land, and on small animals such as rabbits, antelopes and kangaroos, which they hunt with bows and arrows or spears. The harshest deserts provide very little food, so the hunter-gatherers usually live in small groups.

△ The Bushmen of the southern African deserts are among the most skilled hunters in the world. Even so, meat is always scarce in the desert and a kill is always shared among the whole band.

◁ An elderly Aborigine rests beneath a wind-worn rock overhang in the Australian Desert. Many of these caves are believed to be Spirit Places with magical properties. (Try to find out what the white objects are, embedded in the roof of the cave.)

◁ Cattle are a sign of wealth as well as a source of food to the livestock herders of Ethiopia. Unfortunately there are now more cattle than the land can support. They eat everything in sight, turning the dry grasslands into useless desert.

The semi-deserts and dry grasslands have a little more to offer, and these are often the home of nomadic herdsmen. They live in larger groups, building their homes from brushwood, thatch, woven cloth and animal skins, and living on a mixture of gathered foods and the meat and milk of their cattle, sheep and goats.

The aristocrats of the desert nomads are the herdsmen and traders of the Sahara and Arabian Deserts – the Tuareg, Bedouin and other peoples. They too keep goats and sheep, but in their lifestyle and traditions the most important animal is the camel. It provides milk and meat, wool for clothing and tent-making, and leather. Most important of all, it carries the trader across the desert with wool, leather, salt and dates which are traded in more fertile areas for grain.

△ The Bedouin were originally nomadic herdsmen and traders. In recent years many have become more settled, spending part of the year travelling, but settling and cultivating the land during the growing season. This Bedouin encampment was photographed near Jerusalem.

23

# Desert towns and villages

When people first began to build settlements in the desert, their main requirement was a good supply of water. For this reason most desert towns have grown up at oases. Many of the larger towns, with their important markets, are also at the meeting points of ancient desert trade routes.

Land that can be used for crops is far too valuable to build on, so many desert towns follow a similar pattern. Food crops and date palms take up the fertile low ground, while the houses are clustered together on higher, stonier ground.

▽A typical oasis village in the desert of south Morocco. Every bit of land that can be watered from the small stream is used to grow food crops, while the thick-walled houses with their tiny windows occupy the rocky slope at the foot of a barren hillside.

The buildings of a North African desert town are usually made of mud bricks. These soak up the heat by day and release it slowly at night, keeping the occupants warm. The houses are built close together so that the narrow streets are always in deep shadow, out of the Sun's glare.

In the broad belt of dry semi-desert that lines the southern edge of the Sahara, typical villages consist of clusters of round beehive houses of brushwood, or of interwoven sticks plastered with mud and straw. Both give good protection from the fierce daytime heat.

The highland deserts of Central Asia are a complete contrast. Here cold, not heat, is the main enemy. The nomadic herdsmen live in *yurts* – portable houses made of thick felt mats fixed to a wooden frame. The permanent homes of towns and villages are made of wood, earth and stone.

△ Many ingenious machines are used to raise water from a well. This one, used in Egypt, is called a *sakia*.

▽ Mud-plastered walls and thatched roofs are typical of houses in the Sahel area south of the Sahara Desert.

# Technology in the desert

The desert lands do not have a great deal to offer the farmer or livestock owner, but they contain some of the most valuable and important **mineral deposits** on Earth. Gold, diamonds, iron and copper are found here as well as the raw materials for nuclear fuels and the phosphates and nitrates used in making fertilizers.

One of the most important mineral resources is oil. The huge increase in its value in recent years has enabled many desert countries in North Africa and the Middle East to greatly improve the living standards of their people. They have built new roads, schools and hospitals, started new industries, and greatly increased the amount of food that is being grown.

▽ Kharg Island in the Persian Gulf is one of the main loading terminals for tankers carrying crude oil from the Arabian oilfields to the main industrial regions of the world. In recent years operations have been badly hit by the war between Iraq and Iran.

◁ The coastal sands of the Namib Desert contain valuable deposits of diamonds, but huge earthwork dams must be built to protect the excavations from the sea.

The people of the Sahel are less fortunate. They have no oil, or any other mineral wealth, so they are unable to pay for the technology they so urgently need. That is why aid from the richer countries is so important.

Pest control, for example, can make a huge difference to the amount of food that can be produced. Irrigation schemes can bring much more land into use, and careful use of fertilizers can double or even treble the amount of food grown on a hectare of land. Even simple things like food-storage methods are important. Millions of tonnes of grain are lost every year in Africa because people do not know how to store it.

Health care must also be improved, because people who are weakened by hunger and disease have little strength left to work the land.

△A swarm of desert locusts can destroy an entire crop in less than an hour, so the war against these pests is a high priority.

▽Irrigation systems and the use of fertilizers have made the desert green with crops in parts of Israel.

# Deserts on the march

All over the world, forests, woods and marshlands are being taken over for farming and building land. But the most endangered habitats of all are the dry grasslands and semi-deserts. Every year, an area almost as big as Belgium finally loses its few remaining trees and patches of grass and becomes desert. The reason is, quite simply, that these habitats are being overloaded.

One of the main problems is the huge number of people living in these regions. Wood is the only fuel they have for heating their homes and cooking their food. Once all the available dead wood has been collected, the trees are cut down. Once they are gone, there is nothing to protect the soil. It turns to dust and is soon washed away or blown away by the wind.

▽ Nearly half the world's population depends on wood for cooking and heating. In Kenya and in many other arid regions, gathering enough firewood for one day's needs is a back-breaking job that takes up the whole day.

▷ Goats are the most destructive of all man's domestic animals. They are extremely agile and can eat almost anything. By the time they finish, barely a leaf or green shoot will remain on this tree.

28

Arid areas such as the Sahel, the dry plains of India and the semi-deserts of Turkey and Afghanistan can usually support a small number of people and their livestock without permanent damage. When the animals move on, the land has a chance to recover. But when there are too many sheep and goats and cattle, *everything* gets eaten – even the twigs and bark. When rain finally does fall on the parched earth, it is too late. The trees and shrubs and grasses are all dead.

One hope for the future lies in new varieties of trees and bushes that grow quickly in desert soils. As well as protecting the land, they provide fuelwood and thick foliage for animal feed.

▽ Several different kinds of trees and bushes are being used here at En Gedi in Israel to anchor the loose desert soil and make the land productive again.

△ The result of overgrazing. Maasai herdsmen drive their cattle to a water hole across a landscape that has been stripped of all its vegetation.

# Glossary

**Arid** Simply means dry, but when used in geography it means an area with so little rainfall that it has hardly any vegetation.

**Arroyo** A Spanish word for a dry stream bed in a desert region. The stream bed only fills with water after one of the rare desert storms. The same feature in North Africa is called a *wadi*, and in India a *nullah*.

**Atmospheric pressure** The weight of air pressing down on the Earth's surface. It varies from place to place and from time to time because currents of air sometimes rise, which reduces the air pressure, or they fall, which increases the air pressure.

**Butte** A flat-topped, steep-sided hill in the deserts of America and Mexico. It is carved from horizontal layers of rock and is usually a "left-over" of a larger area of high ground (mesa) that has been worn away.

**Calcareous** Describes any rock containing calcium carbonate. The main calcareous rocks are limestone and chalk.

**Crust** The outer layer of the Earth. It is quite thin and rocky and floats on a partly molten layer beneath.

**Deposition** The process in which sand and mud sink to the bottom of a lake, river or ocean.

**Desert** The extreme type of arid area, usually with less than 25 cm (10 in) of rain in a year, and very little vegetation.

**Erosion** The process in which the rocks of the Earth's surface are slowly worn away by wind, rain, rivers and glaciers.

**Evaporate** Change from a liquid into a gas or vapour. A puddle dries up on a warm day because the water evaporates into the air.

**Flash floods** A sudden and violent flood that occurs in a desert when it rains. The ground is so hard the water cannot soak in, so it rushes over the surface in a flood, often causing erosion.

**Gorge** A deep channel cut by a river. The sides are very steep, often vertical.

**Granite** One of the most common rocks of the Earth's crust. It is also one of the most common igneous rocks – those that have formed by the cooling down of molten rock from inside the Earth's crust.

**Gully** (plural gullies) A steep-sided water-worn channel, not as big or deep as a gorge.

△Goatskin tents like this are used by the Tuareg people of Upper Volta. A gap around the base of the tent wall allows the air to circulate.

△Even quite large multi-storey buildings can be made with Sun-baked mud bricks. This painting shows the town of Suq al Ainau in the Yemen.

△To keep out the bitter cold of the Asian winter, the nomads of Mongolia use tents made of thick felt mats attached to a wooden frame.

30

**Habitat** The place where an animal or plant lives. Forest, desert, river bed and marsh are all types of habitat.

**Inselberg** An isolated rocky hill in the middle of an expanse of desert or plain.

**Loess** A very fine soil that is made of material carried by the wind from a desert region a long way away.

**Mesa** A large flat-topped area of land standing higher than the surrounding land. It is usually what remains of an ancient landscape that is in the process of being worn away by erosion.

**Mineral deposit** A geological formation in which one particular mineral is present in large enough quantities to be mined.

**Nocturnal** Means active at night, or mainly at night. Many desert animals are nocturnal, hunting at night and sleeping during the day.

**Nomad** A member of a small group or tribe that has no permanent home, but instead spends life travelling from place to place.

**Oasis** (plural oases) An area in the middle of a desert where there is water at the surface – usually in the form of a well or spring but also sometimes a permanent river.

**Outback** An Australian term for the great wilderness area of the Australian Desert.

**Outwash fan** A large fan-shaped area of sand, gravel or rocks that builds up where a wadi or arroyo flows out on to a flat plain or valley bottom.

**Pollinate** The process of fertilizing a flower so that it can produce seeds. Pollen from the male part of one flower must reach the female part of another flower. In some plants the pollen is carried by the wind, while in many others it is carried by insects as they search for nectar.

**Prevailing wind** This term is used for the wind that most often blows at a particular place.

**Prey** Any animal that is hunted by another animal as a source of food.

**Rain shadow** The region on the downwind side of a hill or mountain range. Because the prevailing winds lose most of their moisture as rain over the hills, the rain-shadow area is dry.

**Salt lake** A lake in a desert or semi-desert region in which the water has a very high mineral salt content. Salt is constantly added to the lake by streams flowing into it, but only *pure* water evaporates from the lake – so the solution gets more and more concentrated.

**Scrub** A type of vegetation consisting of tough woody evergreen plants, 1–2 m (3–6 ft) high, with a few scattered trees here and there.

**Sedimentary** The name used for rocks such as limestone, sandstone and mudstone that were formed from fine sand and mud deposited in water. (Look up **Deposition** as well.)

**Temperate** The word means moderate and is used to describe the climatic zone between the warm tropics and the cold polar regions.

**Trade Winds** One of the main wind systems of the world. There are two sets of Trade Winds. The Northeast Trades blow towards the equator in the northern hemisphere while the Southeast Trades blow towards the equator in the southern hemisphere.

**Tropics** The Tropic of Cancer is a line around the globe, parallel to the equator but at latitude 23½° North. The Tropic of Capricorn is a similar line, the same distance south of the equator. The region between the two is hot throughout the year, and everywhere in this zone has the Sun directly overhead twice in every year.

**Urine** The liquid waste produced by an animal. In desert animals it is often very concentrated and is passed in very small quantities so as not to waste precious water.

**Westerlies** The bands of strong winds lying north and south of the Trade Winds. In the northern hemisphere they blow from the southwest: in the southern hemisphere they blow from the northwest.

# Index

PRINTED IN BELGIUM BY

proost
INTERNATIONAL BOOK PRODUCTION